To Pat

HOLD TIGHT

warmest wishes

x

ALSO BY ALISON CHISHOLM

POETRY *Alone no More* (with Robin Gregory)
Flying Free
The Need for Unicorns
Single Return
Flying Free
Light Angles
Daring the Slipstream
Mapping the Maze

OTHERS *The Craft of Writing Poetry*
A Practical Poetry Course
How to Write Five-Minute Features
The Art of Writing Poetry
(correspondence course)
How to Write About Yourself
(with Brenda Courtie)
Writing Competitions: The Way to Win
(with Iain Pattison)
The Handy Little Book of Tips for Poets

HOLD TIGHT

Alison Chisholm

HEADLAND

First published in 2009
by
HEADLAND PUBLICATIONS
38 York Avenue
West Kirby, Wirral
CH48 3JF

British Library Cataloguing in Publication Data.
A full CIP record for this book is available from the British Library
ISBN: 978 1 902096 54 4

Printed in Great Britain by
Oriel Studios, Orrell Mount
Hawthorne Road
Merseyside L20 6NS

HEADLAND acknowledges the financial
assistance of Arts Council England.

CONTENTS

(Continued)

CHARACTERS

WRITE STUFF

ACKNOWLEDGEMENTS

Some of these poems have appeared in *Acumen, Aspire, Daily Mail, Envoi, Fairy Poems* (Macmillan), *Orbis, Poetry Monthly, Roundyhouse* or *Writing Magazine*, or have been broadcast by *BBC Radio Merseyside*.

'Heir Apparent' won the 2007 Sefton poetry competition, 'Invisible Mending' the 2005, and 'First Day' the 2006 Society of Women Writers and Journalists annual poetry competition, and several poems have been placed in the Ohio Poetry Day and NFSPS contests.

for
Emma and Julia
with love

LIVERPOOL WATERFRONT

These are my birds poised for flight,
petrified, unflappable; one looks over the water,
one guards the city's guts.

My river calms Irish breakers,
laps high town sand,
rusts the cast iron shore.

My ships shuttle, cross and re-cross,
ferry people
who will never walk alone.

My great anchor rests, grounded,
knowing invisible chains
will not let me get away.

THE POEM I'D LIKE TO READ

Don't give me butterflies and buttercups.
I want a poem that can hurt where it bites me.
I want to be punched drunk with hard words,
slapped about by metaphor and simile,
flayed by that nugget that strips the skin.

Keep falling leaves and woodsmoke
for tea-and-scones autumn. I want
poems that sting like absinthe at three a.m.,
poems that crawl into bed at five
and lie till dusk, hungover, not forgotten.

Slam shut the pages of rolling seas, majestic mountains.
Give me a chance to soar and plummet,
tie my mind to a rollercoaster,
burn my fingers on red hot images,
scorch me with the graze of truth's bullet.

Spare me from nature's wonders, the miracle of birth,
the waste of war. Instead, let me ride
uncharted courses to new continents,
align a constellation of undiscovered stars,
learn the how of light; find the missing link.

BLACK WEDNESDAY

Music lessons are six lamp-posts distant;
just far enough to make cycling worthwhile.
I push on pedals, sustain a free-flow
of air streaming my hair, breezing bare arms
to gooseflesh. Tempo slows as I coast
through the narrow black gate, brake, dismount.

I steer straight scales, chains of arpeggios;
sing a fourth above this note, a fifth below that.
Grieg trips; Beethoven crashes - and as the minute hand
limps to complete its circuit,
my Buddha of a teacher rolls
onto the stool, and we synchronise
in tiresome reels of 'Carousel' duets.

Dusk plays into twilight, damps and darkens.
I shiver, wish I'd heeded 'take a coat' advice,
wobble in the saddle, settle
to going-home rhythms. Now the road
is ghosted with shadows. I speed
from pool to pool of bluish light
while my tandem alter ego reaches, stretches,
vaults my head, a cadenza
with five encores.

The final lamp before our house
glimmers the chromatic path
to sanctuary of the shed, back door,
hot chocolate and a coal fire's crescendo.

But still the echoes of a dying chord
throb where my pulse races,
fill voids of dark with fear. I hear
a falling cadence sigh, a wheel spin;
tingle as the clock begins its cycle,
starts the countdown again,
again,
again.

FIRST DAY

First day at school. The teacher's whistle blows.
My Mum is here. I grasp her hand so tight
she has to prise her fingers free. She goes,
abandons me. I bite my lip - don't cry
but taste the sick of fear behind my teeth.
I'm given plasticine and told to play.
I have to tuck my hankie up my sleeve;
keep still and quiet. I want to run away.
I try to write my name. The pencil shakes
and wobbly letters tumble on my book.
I look up at the clock. The big hand takes
an age to creep around its face. I'm stuck.
I'm scared this agony will never pass.
First day at school. I wish it was my last.

PEAPOD DAYS

Remember placing thumb and finger
each side of a sun-warmed green pod?
A squeeze - not too hard,
or the peas would squash -
and a pop released that garden-breath
of summer. You eased your thumbnail
down one seam, hinged the other,
became the first person who had ever seen
those fat spheres of sweetness.

One for the mouth, four for the bowl -
and your fingers rolled them from their moorings
leaving five studs behind. Then you flexed the pod,
turned it inside out, and nibbled,
breaking down elastic fibres
until a soggy emerald mess fell to the grass.

When the bowl was full you'd stand,
stretch feeling back to cramped knees and toes,
sense an ache begin below your ribs,
and know the last ten ... twenty ... fifty peas
had been a mistake.

Indoors the kitchen oozed
with scents of grilling lamb,
warm earthiness of potatoes boiling on the hob,
promises of gravy.

Remember ordinary days like those -
green-gardened, stove bubbling -
when you feel the pod of a train
squeezing as though it will burst,
your feet numb beneath the desk,
office air sickly with over-breathing.

CAPTURING THE MOON

I remember a task
set one drowsy Monday afternoon
before the art teacher shrugged on the wrap
of boredom, of cynicism.

Paint the moon, she said,
but not from your perspective.
Paint it from above, around it
a corona of rainbow light, in a still pool
seen through leafless branches of a sycamore.

Imagination bypassed its habitual slow burn,
leapt and fizzed, darted, rocketed to the moon,
looked back from its vast shadow
into that pool mirror's molten silver;
saw a tapestry of metallic lights
in colours too new to be named.

Excited fingers tingled
as I clasped the brush, washed
thick, woven paper with every subtle shade.

For once I ignored muted conversations,
for once I stayed beyond the bell,
revelled in an orgy of creativity.

For once it worked. My picture hung,
pinned to the artroom notice board;
and my moon lived, glowed pride inside me,
showed how I could get it right.

Since that day, I have seldom felt
such connection, have learned to be content
with paler colours, predictable, staid.
But in rare moments I can glimpse again
black filigree of twigs, and through them
a quicksilver flash of water,
a moon snared and waiting to be conquered.

CHANCE MEETING

I should not have been there
  but
we had to move for my father's work
and I needed a place I could find a friend
and my sister was irritating
and my mother nagged
and I was fifteen and filled with hate
and I wanted to rebel
and I ended up at the after-show party

you should not have been there
  but
you dropped out of college and went back home
and you needed a place you could go to think
and your brothers were childish
and your father nagged
and you were twenty and filled with despair
and you wanted to go your own way
and you ended up at the after-show party

  and
thirty-nine years a mortgage two kids
and a whole lot of love later
I still can't work out how we chanced to meet

HOUSEWARMING GIFT

We lived in this house three days
before we explored deep garden beyond the fence;
three days of emptying boxes,
surprised by every unchipped piece of china,
a patina of newsprint on our hands.
The woven strips of wood, man tall,
were not our boundary. Slipping between their overlap
we learned the lives of our predecessors.

Two bicycles, rusted, saddles mildewed,
nestled in last summer's rotted clippings;
a gas cooker, blue mottled, black bruised
on its white enamel oven door,
basked in memories of cottage pie,
Sunday roast, egg-and-bacon breakfasts.
March-rained cardboard boxes skulked,
a pair of faded lilac curtains backdropped
sprays of leaves, of twigs. Decay's musk
cast its mournful blanket over all.

To load these sad reminders - of three lives
transported half a world away -
into a skip, would seem betrayal. So instead
we dug deep, fashioned
a communal grave, committed
fabric, cuttings, artefacts to ground,
let them sink through sandy soil
to settle, packed earth tightly over them.

Today the fence is gone. A holly tree,
bluebells, rose campion, cowslips
consecrate the garden's end. Beneath,
the essence of those lives still leaches, disperses,
edging back and up and through foundations,
grafting its gift.

THE LIVING ROOM

This is the room where I lay on the floor,
stared at ochre walls, bottle green ceiling,
knew I'd come home.

This is the room I painted, beached-whale naked,
six hours before giving birth,
and where I fed-and-changed-and-fed-and-changed
my twenties away.

This is the room where I cried when the cat died,
the hamster died,
my uncle died,
father died,
mother died,
and when the cheese and onion pie burned.

This is the room whose walls saw me eat,
saw me diet, a seesaw from ten to sixteen.

This is the room where Puccini one-fine-day-ed,
the Monkees hey-hey-ed
and Brookside Close changed my life.

This is the room which has groaned
when the crossword wouldn't fit
and the knitting unravelled,
and the cat ran across the Scrabble board.

This is the room where I make poems,
make Christmas cards,
make friends, make earrings, make love.

This is the room where the family roots
no matter how far branches stretch,
leaves scatter, no matter
what strange walls support its boughs.

HIGHWAY ROBBERY

April. Expecting to be fooled
we take your call prepared to banter - foiled
by news of your heart attack.
Black ribbon of road tars funeral thoughts,
threads the three-hour journey,
robbing precious time we need for you.

May. We by-pass Spring, don't stop, don't stare -
scarcely note the skip of lambs,
new green of trees; for now your by-pass
has stolen wits and movement at a stroke.

June. The car has learned its track,
knows grooves of its own passing
as our visits stretch, seeps rubber from tyres
to mark its way. And we spend whole days
getting there and getting back,
squeezing your ticking visits in between.

July. We travel silently, for now
our route conceals new dark. As you rally,
we carry flowers another mile to where
friends grieve. We curse the way for stealing
all our certainty, forbidding happy-ever-afters.

August. Trying new routes, car filled with flower fumes,
we stumble on straight roads that promise
more miles, less time. Their ease demands a forfeit,
and when sleep nods a drift toward the fast lane
we surrender confidence; know more of fear.

September. All the lambs are grown or gone,
and first autumn glints tinge leaves.
You are stronger, but these ways have weakened us,
our essence sapped as oil sucked from the earth
which cannot be replaced. The road drums
beneath our wheels. This journey bleeds us bare.

BITING POINT

I reverse into the space
between last lessons and nightschool,
tick over as you slide books and files
on the back seat. I am the buffer
absorbing shocks of amended timetables,
hasty meetings, another nervous breakdown.

Click of the indicator syncopates
with intermittent wipers, and crunching over conkers
reminds how fall's stopwatch starts to speed.

An amber light drizzles its warning.
Slowing past Woolworths allows a glimpse
of September's first Christmas trees,
hints at smells of coin and oranges,
insists 'Do they know it's ....' guilt trips.
Green light. First gear. I feel the biting point:
accelerate.

LEARNING SALT

The simple act of kneeling in the sea
needs concentration, as clown-shoe fins flap,
weight of water pounds against her chest.
She breathes by suck and blow, a primitive response
to lungs' vacuum, must learn to trust by holding breath,
sweeping her mouthpiece to arm's length and back.

She tries, swallows brine, fumbles, splutters to air, tries again.
At last, mouth clogged with salt, she manages.

Now her reward surrounds her, fish
that move above, beneath her
shimmer her fingers, lock glances through the mask.
Following the fall of sand and rock
she finds jade secrets, weed and wrack,
fingers shells, pebbles, keeps breathing
suck and blow. This is her element -

but air and sun conspire to draw her back.
Now she is fighting, battles the thrust
compelling her upward, strains to find
a route to soothe with sea anemones,
to drift with angels and with cuttlefish.

She has to clear the tube, removes her mouthpiece,
makes the fatal error: breathes.

And she is gasping, gulping
sea and salt into her lungs; but groping
does not find air - light above is still
too dim, too green - she lunges upward.

Rush of day shocks. She chokes,
spits sea as she splits the surface.
Salt crazed, she cannot move,
floats on waves until harsh sun
begins to prickle; paddles to the cove,
lets water drag her over pebbles, beached.

Later, life later, she stands an hour
beneath her shower's drizzle
in control of water, feeling it slide
down breasts and back, legs, arms,
feeling it wash sea's crystals from her hair.

Still the tang stings her lips; and now,
late and last, tears come, and she learns salt.

COMMUNICATION

You wrote me letters, black inked, line on line
with details of your day, your feelings, scrawled
in your familiar hand. We bridged the time
between our meetings with those endless calls,
content to simply feel each other breathe
a telephone apart. Then e-mail brought
the power to rush your written words to me,
span cyber-space at half the speed of thought.
Text messaging crunched language, but its code
was easy to decipher, for I knew
the route your mind would follow, and I could
interpret icons drawing me to you.
   But clearest of them all, I understand
   Your fingers tracing kisses on my hand.

ALL THAT JAZZ

Let us gorge on the gift of bits and pieces,
a drawer's medley of lace and lipstick,
pocket knives, candles and string;
a percussion of buttons and needles,
pots, pans and spoons, wrench and hammer.

Let us relish the richness of letters and postcards,
cacophony of pens and pencils
spilling from their tin, and the wail
of the cellphone, CD player, laptop and palmtop,
backtracked with siren and rattle and trainswish.

Let us sigh with content at offbeat syncopation
of trips to the zoo, cabarets, park strolling,
dog walking, diving through breakers
and lying in bed with a velvet voiced
case of champagne.

Let us give ourselves up to the double bass,
trombone, the drums and the trumpet,
the clarinet, saxophone, off-key piano
that weave life's sweet music
and all that jazz.

POST MORTEM

There will be a chunk of Cheddar
and three bottles of Moet
in the fridge. Five down will tantalise
with empty squares, while a layer of dust
drifts the window. A final chapter
will not have the chance
to exonerate the butler;
and a dentist will sigh
over another missed appointment.

Bulbs may conspire
in underground activity, not realising
the uselessness of resisting late frost.
New potatoes could slough their soft skin,
marry rivulets of butter,
but never learn the consummation of teeth.
Birdsong will pierce the dusk,
disappear unheard.

There will be seas I have not sailed,
roads I have not taken,
mountains that have not visited me.
There will be countries and continents
that will not know my foot's impression.

I close my eyes, a peek-a-boo child,
know that the world cannot see me,
wonder if it will still be there
when they are opened.

THE FULL PICTURE

To know part of the story
means edging from bliss ignorance
into a half way hell. Princesses
sleep for ninety years, glass slippers
never find their owner;
boys grow fatter in a witch's oven
and the wolf still lurks in Grandma's bed.
Before flames start to lick your feet
let truth trickle in a prince's kiss,
pair the odd scraps of learning,
grasp a hand to pull you clear
and cut your monster in a thousand pieces.
Then your dreams, fleeting and impotent,
will cage your ogres, dungeon them,
allow you the full picture.

BITING BACK

This is a stick-up -
hands above your head.
This banana is loaded.

For too many years
you have seen fresh fruit
as the soft option. We have watched
while you squeezed pomegranates,
poked plums, ripped
green fringes from innocent strawberries.

Today it's our turn
to sniff you, prod you;
to decide whether you are worthy
of placing us in your fruitbowl.

A legion of oranges,
with grapes and raspberries protecting their rear,
is poised to attack.

Surrender now.
Resistance is futile.
The melons have you covered.

AFTERWARDS ...

It is difficult to know what to say
so I observe that the bubbles
in the centre of the cup of coffee
rotate more quickly than those around the edge.
I learn this is physics, and drag and velocity figure.
Knowing the theory could not prepare me
for those clinging globes of air hugging the cup,
each reflecting curved images of lips
poised to blow the drink cool;
could not prepare me for the Dervish dance
spinning at the middle.
Taking a sip whisks the foam to confusion
where big bubbles, small bubbles weave intricate patterns,
a shift of balance.
I put down the cup, stir the coffee again, watch:
equilibrium restored, the bubbles in the centre
rotate more quickly than those around the edge.

But we can never undo what nearly happened,
never untaste the first sip's chaos.

PIETÀ

See where marble fell away,
revealing at its heart
the world's core: for here
this body broken for us all
is muscled in stone, veined
where rock itself pulses, wrapped
in petrified folds.

Look further: see beyond pale flesh
and focus where a mother's downcast gaze
pierces the soul's centre. Let her grief
start tears behind your eyes
as if your son - scourged, tortured, crucified -
freezes in your arms.

This moment encapsulates eternity,
fixes the cost of reconciliation;

and it is here, where sightless eyes angle
through neverending pain, you learn
the strength of woman.

Her hands that fed and dressed a child
support his wounded side, gesture
a need to understand. Her lap,
where an infant smiled, cradled safe,
holds his dead weight. Her lips
that kissed away his tears are set,
closed firm against a hint
of pity or complaint.

She is unyielding; her power is absolute
and incorruptible. Look again
where woman's essence stirs the very air,
to see where marble weeps and bleeds.

RESURRECTION

Imagine a valley littered with bleached bones -
sternum, rib, patella, tibia, skull -
flesh long decomposed, or torn by vultures;
and in that place of death and terror's shadow,
imagine being asked if those bones could live again.

Now hear the first faint tap of metatarsal,
clicks then clatters, crashes
as bone on bone reforms, reconstitutes
until a skeleton stands before you.

You are beyond terror: can only watch
as muscles, sinew, tendon reappear
as skin clothes the apparition,
turns the structure to an almost man.

Almost - for though you look to see
if this phenomenon could live,
no air inflates its lungs, no exhalation shows.

Then last, most strange of all, the trinity
of wind, breath, spirit animates this body,
and those dried bones are quick.

You stand transfixed. You know
the intervention you have seen
cannot be mortal, has to be divine,
will fill your nightmares, haunt your waking hours,
will colour thinking till the day you die.

THREE O'CLOCK FEARS

Three o'clock. Sleep groggy, you grope
an automatic route to the bathroom, half doze
until water's cold shock snaps your hands.

You search a reason for waking: traffic, perhaps,
the need to pee, gusts of rain against your window.
Forget the dream, don't think about the dream.

You lie on your back, feel your heart's thud
vibrate the mattress; resent the cat
who stands, settles, and is already sleeping.

You turn on your side. Grey, dead fingers reach
from your dream, edge around the curtains.
Don't think. Recite a nursery rhyme,

times table, family tree. Work the list
of mental narcotics ... bank statement,
shopping, counting sheep.

Reach for the radio; it will soothe
in lazy syncopations. Half past three.
Forget the dream, don't think about the dream.

Your eyelids are heavy: but something disturbs.
You hear the tread and creak
of footstep and staircase, feel movement in room's air.

Outside a crescent moon stabs at your window,
branches lattice shadows on your drapes.
If your eyes open you will let it in.

Four o'clock. You are rigid, hardly a breath
shimmering your immobility.
But sleep starts knotting up your mind.

Unseen, undead creatures climb the stairs;
nightmare fingers clutch your bedclothes;
in fields of fear the sheep are massing.

WATCHING THE WEATHER

It is a calm of newspaper and knitting.
I glance at you in the lull,
feel familiar surge of love
the blackest cloud cannot obliterate.
I fear tempests and undercurrents,
watch for signs of gathering storm,
know the turmoil of darkened brows,
thunder rumbling through your head,
blast and deluge.
      There is peace tonight -
your day a pool of quiet,
your journey tranquil. Yet in the deeps
unseen eddies swirl and rise,
choke you, menace. I watch for jagged streaks
that flash your eyes, listen
for crescendoes as pressure builds.
      Knit one, purl one
creates a wary mantra. Your newspaper
stiffens, dips. I am braced, ready
for the hail you hurl, chant silent
love you-s before the surface shatters.

END OF THE ARGUMENT

And when there are no words left
or their hollowness cramps silence,
I look away, stare at the next table,
next chair shedding rust crumbs
that tang grey gravel.

I cannot bear to be here; want to melt
into the table's fan of wrought iron,
to squeeze through the niche
between chair's legs and seat.

I want to become a browned leaf,
cornflake-crisped, ready to dance
at the wind's whim. I want to slide
down a slender green blade,
flake into roots of the sparse grasses.

But I am fixed, locked in this place,
cannot stir, cannot rise
and limp back into the sun.
Your face slabs its defiant glare,
turns the space between us
from table top to prison wall

and I can hear the clanging shut of doors.

HOT WATER

I watch water's column
freefalling to the kettle,
swirling through its element.

> Last time I filled this kettle
> I was making tea for two -
> the old song mocks.

I press my hands
to the smooth white jug,
white as a wedding dress.

> Does she wear white for him?
> Does she wear lace and dancing shoes,
> Estee Lauder and silk sheets?

My palms are burning, but I cannot let go.
If I can keep hold of this scalding whiteness
perhaps he'll come back.

> I can hear him laughing, hear her laughing,
> loud as the rumble of water boiling my hopes
> into steam, loud as the pain scything my fingers.

WHAT IF ... ?

What if he still hasn't learned
not to leave dirty socks on the floor,
how to scramble eggs,
that bath rings don't simply disappear?

What if he still thinks
a bunch of flowers excuses anything,
tickets for the football are a cool date,
Do I look fat in this requires an honest answer?

What if he still prefers
to wake up to heavy metal,
white bread to wholemeal,
his mother's apple pies to mine?

What if he still tries to convince me
the traffic delayed him - not the bar,
he really really wants children ... one day,
he chose his PA for her keyboard skills?

What if my heart still beats faster
when he says my name,
when he smiles and his eyes laugh,
when he just walks in the room?

Yes, my Darling, of course I'll marry you again!

Did I say that out loud?

DAD

I always thought my Dad was Superman.
He knew all the answers,
helped with homework - everything but French -
and ran at superspeed. (Well, faster than me.)

His x-ray vision
could see where my toys needed mending,
and whether I had washed
behind my ears.

He was very brave and very strong,
and not frightened of anything,
not even Kryptonite.

He invented games and puzzles,
made bagatelle boards and dolls' houses.
He could sing and play chess,
or hang wallpaper
faster than a speeding bullet.

Sometimes I would try to squint
between the buttons of his shirt
looking for the telltale letter S.
Seeing didn't matter.
I knew my Dad was Superman.

DIVIDED

I sit and hold your hand. You take the first
slow steps toward the bridge that spans the cleft
between our breathing world and death. Bereft
before the monitors have stilled, I thirst
to follow you, grip tighter, unrehearsed
in solitary limbo. I am left
not comprehending how death's stinging theft
of you can leave me living, lost and cursed.

I know the bridge you cross will carry you
into the next dimension of your faith -
unswerving, steady as the Rock who stands
to greet you. But I tremble at this new
reality, grasp vainly for your wraith,
squeeze life's last warmth from quickly cooling hands.

MUM'S DRESS

I am wearing my mother's dress today.
It is bold and gold, shiny yellow,
a concatonation of hibiscus against
crimson, purple, turquoise;
a shout of jade leaves
on in-your-face black and white.

I am wearing my mother's dress today,
warm on my skin, warm from her skin,
glowing confidence instead of merely gleaming
among the greys and blacks
in my wardrobe.

I am wearing my mother's dress today,
loud enough to shout to the world,
smooth as the touch of hand to forehead,
smart as Sunday best.

I am wearing my mother's dress today,
vibrant from quickstepping
close and parallel movements
a mirror of Dad's, smiling
beyond the camera and into my living room
from that last holiday.

I am wearing my mother's dress today.
It's shorter than I like;
elastic stretches too far at the waist,
tight sleeves dig into my arms.
It's my second skin.

INHERITANCE

These are the hardest gifts to have -
the formal trappings listed in your will,
unwanted presents that cannot be returned.

Instead I treasure mementos beyond money -
the tiny china dog from your dressing table,
battered tablespoon, your favourite vase.
I try your rings and feel your love
entwine my fingers, wear your wrap
to sense your arms around me.

I use the skills you taught me,
typing without a glance at the keyboard,
but being ready to laugh when I go wrong;
crocheting sweaters, tablemats and knickknacks,
prepared to unpick when the pattern muddles.

I keep your habits; make sure
the kitchen's clean and tidy before bed,
tomorrow's books and papers wait in the hall
avoiding morning rush, letters
of thanks are written, invitations answered.

Most precious are shared memories,
the parties, lunches, shopping trips,
jokes and giggles - and, to my surprise,
the way your face looks back more clearly
each time I glance in the mirror.

GIFT

The cat cannot believe my ingratitude.
Instead of stroking sleek ginger flanks and stripy tail,
I yell and lock the door on him,
turn to inspect his gift.

A hollowed sphere of slender twigs and grass
is woven so tightly, no breath of breeze could penetrate.
Inside, hair and drift of cotton are threaded,
softest cushion to cradle the cache of eggs;
outside a lace of moss veils stalk and frond.

Each egg, no larger than a marble,
is painted buttercream, stippled
with oak brown freckles. One has cracked,
and at the fissure in its shell
a tiny, folded form appears,
limbs that will never uncurl,
wings that will not learn feathers.

I wonder if the mother, terrified,
spread her small warmth to clothe them,
or if a sudden snatch of claw
stopped her breath before fear could start.

I wonder if her mate, dispossessed,
is searching through the hawthorn hedge,
not knowing where or how.

I cannot bear to shroud
nest, broken body, eggs
in kitchen paper winding sheets.
Instead I place them gently
in the long grass,
leave them to return to earth
grounded with worm and beetle.

The cat licks pussy-willow paws,
wipes his cheek and whiskers,
purrs.

OLLY

For curling, teddy-bear-soft, in a ball
of ginger and lemon fur
to sleep and sleep and sleep;
For always finding the one person
who hates cats
and sitting on their lap;
For stopping, startled, in the middle
of your wash, one leg
stiff in air;
For the ballet dance, points and pirouette,
while you throw and catch
your purple catnip toy;
For occupying more of the duvet
than your fragile weight
can - logically - achieve;
For sneaking titbits from my plate
and smearing sauce
on the pale carpet;
For purring warm
in my ear,
in my heart;

      I give you cream and fish,
      shelter, and more hugs
      than any cat can count.

FREDDY

He crept into our life,
a small white ghost, soot-spotted,
who discovered our catflap. At first
we only saw a glimpse
of his retreating shadow.

He grew bolder, found the cosy chairs,
ventured deeper into rooms
where other cats snoozed by fires.
Instead of sly mouthfuls,
he helped himself to bowls of food.

November came before he let us touch,
when first frost made him shiver.
I dared to pick him up,
felt his slight weight melting in my arms.

Now he is fixed,
has his favourite spot before the hearth,
circles in front of me,
leads me to the kitchen,
imperious miaows demanding snacks
of cheese or chicken.

His coarse fur is softer.
He sleeps with both eyes shut,
wakes, stretches, strolls
to greet the other cats with nuzzles, licks.

An uninvited guest,
he has become
the centre of our family,
bright greeting of our morning,
our focal point.

MANICURE

She says nothing as I take her hand,
flex fingers, rest her palm on mine.
I am filing her nails, easing minute specks
to dust the carpet. Her skin is parchment,
bones bird-brittle. I am afraid
the slightest pressure could crush her.

She does not speak until I ease her cuticles,
define arthritic fingers with a slick of cream.
'Thank you,' she whispers, 'thank you.' Then:
'I haven't had a manicure for years.'

This is the moment I realise
I have never touched her hands before,
never known the warmth of fingertips
that explored the silk of new born skin,
traced baby eyes and cheekbones, nose and lips;
that knitted intricate sweaters,
peeled and chopped carrots, potatoes, parsnips;
that caressed a lover's tautly muscled frame.

And in the intimacy of buffing her nails,
massaging oil into cracked knuckles, I know
this moment is a tiny celebration,
needs to recognise the link
not of mother-in-law and her son's wife,
but woman to woman, one to one.

I push her colourless varnish aside,
reach in my bag for crazy silver with sparkling flecks,
paint in bold strokes until her fingers flash
indomitable diamond messages,
feel new strength surging through her hands.

TOUCHING ANGELS

Today it rained feathers;
cloud on cloud splitting, sending
white swirls to heap in gardens,
drift down passageways.

There was no sound
as we waded through them, just
a warm vibration in the air,
a scent of music.

Everywhere people were stooping
to scoop up handfuls, light
as mist, heavy as promises.
But at first touch they melted,

leaving nothing behind
except an emptiness of arms,
the silence that remains
when an angel choir stops singing.

STAR

Born of cosmic dust
before dust was,
propelled by the Creator's hand,
I went spinning through space;
and when reverberations
from that first cacophony subsided,
only dark and silence whirled around me.

More ancient than light,
more ancient than time,
I traced a plotted course
while stars wheeled
from dense knot of matter
to white dwarf, to supernova.

Every inch along my route
was planned. I flashed
through unimaginable depths of gas,
of specks that would be planets.

Then at last
my journey brought me just light centuries
from where a blue-green globe
had started breathing, birds flew, insects crawled,
and man reared up to walk on two legs.

I travelled nearer, nearer,
heard within the rock that was my heart
a countdown move inexorably on.
I flared and blazed,
knowing somehow I was near my target.

I became aware
of alien voices urging friends to follow,

a trek of camels plodding mile on mile.
I paused and hovered,
stayed in their sights,
hesitated over palaces,
then stopped above
a dingy cavern, rough-hewn in stone.

Now purposeless and route-less,
I hung in air
vibrating with new sounds,
spilling angel music. And I knew
my fate was not implosion,
not the nothing of black holes.

At last, the hand that first set me in motion
wrapped itself around me,
squeezed until I crumbled back to dust,
and let each atom fall onto this earth,
this planet, baby-blessed,
this place of love.

CHRISTMAS MEMORIES

Do you remember endless days,
school over, Christmas not quite come,
and how you would search the house
for packages that might be yours?

Do you remember cutting pastry shapes,
the stickiness of mincemeat on your fingers,
pricking shortbread with a fork,
making holly leaves from marzipan?

Do you remember last-minute shopping,
jostling crowds with bulging baskets,
tinsel blazing from every window
and slushy snow that chilled through your shoes?

Do you remember Christmas Eve,
breathless anticipation that stole your sleep,
dim tantalising shapes at the foot of your bed,
and skeins of stars through your curtains?

Do you remember raiding your stocking
before it was light, freezing fingers
pulling out pencils and plasticene,
gleaming coins, an apple, an orange?

Do you remember a mountain of parcels,
ripping ribbons from jigsaws, rollerskates,
drawing books, warm woolly cardigans,
and piling your presents up higher and higher?

Do you remember the toys and laughter,
games and chocolates, jokes and crackers?
If you do, try to recapture the child's excitement,
and carry the magic around in your heart.

JANUARY THOUGHTS

Week one: lift Santa from the roof,
wrap silver garlands, pack up glass and crystal,
burn dried out evergreens, and stand the tree -
a monument to festival's excess -
outside your door. Where cards were hung
the walls are bare and dusty.

Week two: time to forget your resolutions;
pizza tempts you from the diet,
and hours you would have spent with lonely neighbours
disappear, lured by shopping mall, TV.
When you resolved weekly visits to the gym,
you should have thought it through.

Week three: the bills arrive, and pound signs
dance inside your sleeping eyes. What happened
to intentions to downsize? When
did the panic, top-price buying overtake
the reassuring 'thoughts that count'?
How could such legions of bottles empty?

Week four: the car's frozen every morning;
even the ducks are shivering. Summer holidays are more
than twenty weeks away. Stamp your boots dry,
fill the house with smells of fires and coffee -
but before you slam the door, see snowdrops, crocus;
smile at the promise of tulips.

CONTACT LENS

I am fragile, frailer than eggshell,
shirt-button small, almost invisible;
handle me with care. Your closest companion,
I collaborate with eye and brain
to make the world clear to you.

I am weightless, so slight
I can slide beneath your eyelid
and you cannot feel me;
but if you turn too fast and let me slip,
I let you know.

I am jealous. When a mote of dust
insinuates itself between my curve
and your eyeball's angle
I sear you with pain, make
those traitor eyes flood.

I am all-knowing, share your secrets,
accompany you every moment,
know where you have been, what you have done.
When you tell the world a different story,
I stay silent.

I am precious, guardian of your greatest gift,
upholder of your vanity. I collude
when you need to sparkle; I ask for nothing,
work through every waking hour.
Treat me well.

INVISIBLE

Something was different. I was floating above my bed -
not in a clichéd euphemism of death,
just lacking the substance of a body.
I was not surprised. I am a wife, a mother,
I know how it feels to be unseen. Curiosity
made me examine the pillow's indent,
smell a whisper of soap and sweat on sheets.

I got to work early, not having to bother
with all that tiresome showering, dressing,
making breakfast, guilt-tripping its calories.
Nobody noticed my not-quite-hands
skimming computer keys, or wondered
at the ghost procession of images flickering the screen.

Taking an early lunch was easy.
No-one saw my non-presence
slipping from the room, or heard
my non-heels tapping down the corridor.

In the park, I tried to feel
the bench's hard wood slats. It was a strange sensation,
almost contact, living within that fractional moment
before lips meet to kiss.

Thinking he was on his own, a man in a dark blue suit
threw his sandwich wrapper on the ground,
picked his nose, and belched.

That was the instant I decided
not to go back to the office, but instead
to try something my body would never dare.
Having little imagination, I chose
the bank. It seemed only fair to call out

This is a raid and, searching memory,
stick 'em up. Nothing happened. I edged
into forbidden territory behind the counter.
No-one shivered in the breeze as I passed.

Childhood's threat that *God can see you*
when Mummy can't echoed in the vault.
I nearly-fingered a stack of notes; put them down,
and, to be contrary but minimise the sin,
helped myself to four paperclips
which danced in air at hand height.

Emboldened by my foray into crime,
I took a free ride home on the bus,
air-kicked the heads off next door's roses,
feigned a finger at the woman opposite.
It was not so much that I hate flowers or nosy neighbours,
more the exhilaration of being able
to do precisely what I liked that captivated me.

I had two hours to play with
before the kids would come squalling home,
another before my husband slammed his briefcase down.
I'd have to work out a story.
I spent a minute looking in mirrors,
tried a few party tricks, pouring water from jug to glass,
making coins disappear. Then I sat down
and switched on TV.

In that moment I realised
how pathetic my little life had become,
how sad. This new freedom
had flooded ordinary tasks and dreams
with light so uncompromising
it turned my form-less self shame-naked,
showed my shallows, un-personed me.

I didn't need to worry about inventing a story.
Long before the others came home I felt
familiar weight of flesh, looked down to see
expected flabby thighs, broken fingernails.
By the time I was standing in the kitchen cooking tea,
listening to inconsequential *how's your day been?* answers,
it was as though nothing out of the ordinary had happened.

But since then I have never been the same.
My head is full of all I would do, if .....
I am a living conspiracy theory, crave expiation,
have been known to weep openly at the smallness
of four paperclips.

FAIREST OF THEM ALL

I remember bud,
pink-tinged blossom,
the first slight swell
then a burst of fibres, seed and core,
plumping with juice, painted with gold flashes,
slowly turning red, rich red.

The shock of being plucked
reminds my instinct of its apple lore -
I must tempt and please and nourish.
I am tumbled with others of my kind,
know their flesh, realise
we are near the climax of our purpose.

Now I am resting in a glass bowl,
smooth and cool, still life
on an ebony table. Anticipation
fevers as long fingers, thin, bejewelled,
stroke the others - curve around me.

I wait for first bite's ecstasy;
feel instead
a needle probing to my core,
slow drip that stings, corrodes.
I know my peel glows ruby still,
know my centre is corrupted.

I am thrust in the dark
of a black coat's pocket,
hurtled along, jolting against
a jut of hip.

Her purpose is strong.
There is no hesitation as she strides,

no change of pace
until she stops and I hear
familiar birdsong, wind in branches;
then a rapping at the door.

Voices murmur, fingers fumble the pocket,
and I am in the light, offered on an outstretched palm.

We are alone,
I and a girl

whose cheeks are my image,
whose eyes are dark and soft as bees.

She lifts me to parted lips.
Cloud-white teeth pierce me,
I am agony of fulfilment, ecstasy of pain.

Something is wrong. Despoiled flesh
fills her mouth, begins
its countdown to destruction;
but she is numbed, cannot speak,
falls before she swallows.

And I am here still, trapped
in the blood red of her throat,
aware of heartbeats slowing, weakening.
And I can only hope for miracles,
send silent messages to thrum the air,
calling all handsome princes in the area
to stop and kiss, dislodge me
before I am the death of her.

SNAKEBITE

It's nearly lunchtime. Every week
I take a little snack. At first
a fieldmouse sufficed, an egg, a few small grubs;
but then I grew. My appetite
increased, and I found rats, then baby rabbits.

Swallowing was not a problem.
If my mouth seemed small
I simply eased it wider. I could force
my jaw to open further, further -
and my length's elastic took lunch whole.

Sometimes my food day came and went
without a morsel crossing my path; no matter,
I could defer my feed for hours. But then
when more days passed I travelled further, risked
dangerous ground beside the settlement.

Once I came across a full-size chicken,
swallowed it in a great gulp. My taste
for such exotic food increased. Next
was a small cat, its furry tail
tickling down my throat.

The dog took longer to ingest,
longer still to digest.
But it was worth the effort,
rich and succulent,
nourishing me for a full ten days.

I have grown more than I ever expected,
appetite swelling exponentially. I have already chosen
next week's lunch. It's small
and pink, wriggles and coos to itself.
They leave it outside in a pram.

SITTING PRETTY

It's difficult to perch for hours
and pose as 'seated nude.'
My neck's all stiff, my leg's gone dead -
and though I'm not a prude
I don't like Leonardo's leer.
He shrugs, looks down his nose;
but from this angle I can see
a stirring in his hose.

Now sitting's hardly flattering
to my maturing figure.
I have to keep my bottom clenched
or else I'd look much bigger.
I have to hold my stomach in,
flex muscles in my chest
to stop my boobs from drooping down
at gravity's behest.

There's nothing much to think about
while staring into space.
I've looked at all the pictures
he's got cluttering the place.
He showed me his cartoons,
but I don't see how they are funny.
I'll try to think up novel ways
to spend my husband's money.

He wanted me immortalised,
but when he sees me bare
I guess he'll change his mind and hide
the thing away somewhere.
I bet he'll make poor Leo paint
a veil to shroud me, while
he crops the canvas at my chin.
The thought just makes me smile.

BEYOND EDEN

The pain of banishment was hard to bear;
I wept to hear the garden gates clang shut -
but now I know the meaning of despair.

I knew - while serpents writhed my dreams, and prayer
found no response - I must be punished; but
the pain of banishment was hard to bear.

My sons brought laughter, filled the empty air;
they raced and swam, found figs and fish and nuts;
but now I know the meaning of despair.

Grown up, one tended fields with spade and share,
the other watched our beasts, helped me forget
the pain of banishment. But I must bear

a deeper hurt. Cain scythed a vicious tear
and Abel's blood cascaded from the cut;
so now I know the meaning of despair.

My heart is split - half slain and half the slayer -
each beat a dart of grief that stabs my gut.
The pain of banishment was hard to bear,
but now I know the meaning of despair.

DIRECTIVES

I have my instructions.
I may not water my lawn with a garden hose,
eat an apple while driving,
smoke in public.
I may not chastise my child,
and will be informed if the government
thinks he's obese.
I can be prosecuted
for failing to sort kitchen scraps from general garbage,
exceeding the speed limit,
expressing politically incorrect opinions
(even in the privacy of my own home.)
I am told how much I can drink,
how many vegetables to eat every day,
that I must cut my salt consumption.
I cannot come into contact
with any child who is not my own
unless the police have certified
that I am not a criminal.
I may not wish my neighbours a happy Christmas
in case it offends their religious beliefs.

Thank God
I live in a free country.

MORNING

It's a gift, unplanned, unchosen,
not asked for but expected.
It's the clean page to be filled
with tiny, neat print
or joyous scribble.
It's pale gold spilling through curtains,
trilling with birdsong,
opening buds of gorse and apple blossom.
It's a well, chilly with fern and moss,
ready to yield floods
of gossip, pain, trouble and passion.
It's honey spread on toast,
it's bacon, the morning bus to work.
It's the chance to change *if only*
to *I will.*
It's the backcloth to conversations
we cannot imagine,
to surprises we cannot dream,
to kisses, country walks,
the last cigarette,
the need to eat four Mars bars.
It's being alive.

UPSIZING

I am sick to see
those skin-bone waifs,
be told their angles make a perfect shape.

I want broad hips to mould a cradle
wide and safe to hold my unborn child.
I want my thighs to cushion
comfort for the baby on my lap,
arms fleshed to hug him safe.
I want soft, padded buttocks
that will fill a chair,
ease my sitting; a rolling stomach
to relish good food's gift. I want
plump cheeks to swell in smiles,
full lips for luscious kisses,
breasts bigger than my lover's hand
can hold.

I will not succumb to urging
to crimp myself in gripping underwear,
shed pounds to make my skeleton protrude,
become a stick, a non-person.

I will be real.
I will be me.

A DRINK WITH GEORGE

A place for lovers? Yes, this suits me well -
the Signorinas are a pretty crew,
obliging, keen to satisfy a man;
but if you think that's all I had in mind,
you're much mistaken. Marble palaces,
reflected in the water's depth, attract;
the Bridge of Sighs, Saint Mark's, and narrow strips
of land all linked by city's arteries
are worth a visit. May we sit awhile?
The leg, you know, makes too much walking hard.
Let's take a glass of wine and watch the world
glide past. At night, when fewer boats are out,
I've started swimming in the Grand Canal.
(I take a lighted brand, a torch to warn
the gondoliers.) Will you swim too, my friend?
The city is a different place by night -
a gaudy tapestry of girls and whores.
Yes, one is special to me, I confess ...
a dark-eyed olive beauty who's content
to leave her husband quietly at home
while she will grace my bed. No, that's not all
that keeps me occupied. Each day I join
a group of holy men whose brotherhood
makes welcome those who wish to talk or think.
Perhaps you'll come with me. If all goes well
you'll need their absolution. Just one thought:
the plague is rife. When walking through the town
I hold a handkerchief across my mouth.
I think it helps - you'll maybe do the same.
My writing? Look around you - can you see
how poets could not fail to be inspired?
Why, stay here long enough, and you might find
you too pick up a pen, and with your words
attempt to conjure pictures in the mind
of anyone who reads. You've finished? Good.
It's time to let night's revelry begin...

ALMSCLIFFE CRAG

(Almscliffe Crag, in a remote corner of Yorkshire,
was visited - and painted - by J. M. W. Turner)

Why did it have to be here, Turner,
an hour beyond the backside of Yorkshire?
You, who saw art in engines, stations,
cities; could you not have chosen Leeds,
warm with people, busy with coffee shops
and bookstores?
    But no.
        I have to follow your path
along uncompromising twists
of one track roads to where great slabs
of solid rock do not lift the spirit,
where muddy puddles ooze
depressing as dry stone walls.
Did you enjoy hawthorn hedge and dandelion,
field and field - and for a change, another field?
    Find me
        a motorway to gladden my soul,
the welcome of tarmac,
concrete's reassurance. Paint me
the comfort of bus stops and office blocks,
traffic lights, lamp posts, and sweet red mail vans.

CIVIC DUTY: FUERTEVENTURA

Good housewives never burn the fish -
but these wailing widows
take the monstrous cod,
silver foil scales flapping,
mouth a giant O,
and hurl it on the pyre.

Flames flicker past their veils,
light on stubble, dance
on Latin leather skin,
muscled arms. The widows
flap heavy black skirts
to coax golden sparks, fan
new tongues from embers.

And now a rich procession catches up:
white frocked girls, white suited boys
all marching to the band, and clowns
cavort through peering crowds. A yell -
a cheer - and the foil fish
collapses into ash.

Stripping their weeds, the mourning wives
become police chief, mayor, hotelier;
they do not need to hide
from fear of draft, know there is peace
and paella to come, not carnage.

A chirr of castanets: the carnival continues.
Burden of remembrance burns.

MONTAÑA ROJA, FUERTEVENTURA

This is a place of quiet and mystery,
a dead volcano, vast and red with iron.

Its flow lines sculpt rock sides
into the shape and texture of a treetrunk -

but what a tree - the size and scale
of the race of giants who strode here,

of the hero Majorere, his body
ripped apart by murderous gales.

Are his the haunting moans
that freeze the flesh of any walking by?

Where blood red rock meets bleached sand
shell and fossil mix, evidence

of surge of lava, constant pounding of the ocean,
merging to be the spirit of the island.

Go on in silence. Gaze up in awe.
Know you are in the presence of magic.

BEACH BAG

My mother's great white handbag sang
a drunken sailors' chorus of 'O Sole Mio,'
tremolo accompanied by clink
of two warm bottles of spumante.

Tubes of sun lotion spilled from its depths,
and a white flannel billowed in a plastic bag
to bulge the canvas sides clasped
by a broad gold buckle, reflecting sun's glare.

Mum would rummage in its hold to find
a half pack of fruit pastilles,
scarlet Max Factor lipstick, a comb,
spare pair of comfy sandals -

while beneath her searching fingers memories
of sand grains rustled, cotton hankies tacked the breeze,
and distant tales of witch and wizard lurked,
to roll and break at bedtimes.

September sobered summer's end, folded flags
of cotton frocks away in cases: but if we listened
we could hear, anchored in the wardrobe's fathoms,
a rebel bag humming 'That's Amore.'

OLD HOUSES

A presence clings to mortar, wood and stone.
Old houses breathe the resonance of years.
When you're indoors, you're never on your own.

Some trace of every person who has owned
this land before you lingers, reappears -
a presence - clings to mortar, wood and stone.

Walls harbour memories of flesh and bone,
of flakes of skin, and air exhaled, and tears.
When you're indoors, you're never on your own.

More intimate, more strange, an undertone
of person - not quite soul - somehow coheres
as presence; clings to mortar, wood and stone.

And everything that's happened here is known
by rooms and stairs, creates an atmosphere.
When you're indoors, you're never on your own.

If friends and lovers leave you all alone,
embrace walled memories, ignore your fears.
A presence clings to mortar, wood and stone.
When you're indoors, you're never on your own.

DELUGE

The gods emptied buckets. Tourists,
drenched, squelched for shelter,
raced to sanctuary of Roman baths.
Blue-white forks spotlit mosaic floor, alcoves, plunge.

Someone found a bag of sweets,
passed them to strangers - and the gloom dam burst.
A freckle-covered boy zapped hand-held aliens,
two small girls played chase between pillars,
and morose English families
struck up weather conversations.
Holiday humour lifted the unspoken ban,
and two shorts-and-T-shirted men
debated who would win the primaries.

Weather forgotten, cobbled roads
were almost dry before the party broke.

'And in Roman baths,' a bored guide droned,
'the people met, made friends, shared food,
played games, argued politics ....'

LADETTE

Beneath a holly tree,
grass damp, a dandelion
shocks the garden's ordered elegance.
Brash gold sticks out its tongue
at rollered lawns, flirts in the breeze,
raises its skirts to flash green petticoats.
Picked, it starts to darken,
rage fuelling impudence,
outer petals down-turned, petulant,
amber mop at the centre bristling.

If it could speak
it would shout *bollocks*.

NEW TERM: MONDAY: 9 AM

He is an island,
unblinking, unmoving
in a heaving sea of books and sweat and spots.

You been a teacher long, Sir?
Got a girlfriend, Sir?
Got any cigs? Got any dope?

He can handle this. He can handle them.
He remembers the lectures, rôle play,
notes, discussion topics.

What you waiting for, Sir?
Can I go to the toilet, Sir?
This is boring, Sir.

He will find the wavelength,
listen, learn. He won't judge.
He'll be their friend, he'll charm, encourage.

You getting any, Sir?
Tracey'll do you,
she's a slag.

Sit down. Open your books.
Shut up. Shut up.
Shut up. Shut up. Shut up.

EYES TO SEE

It started in a meeting: bored, he drew
a lattice of curved shapes
wrapping and weaving each around each,
defining some with heavy lines, others with shading.
He would have thrown the sheet away -
but when he tried to crumple it
creases curled to form the ghost of a girl.

That night he sketched - and the next, the next -
though drawing was an unlearned skill.
Lines formed a tangle of hair falling to shoulders,
defined mouth and cheek, smoothed a languid hand,
but eyes remained in shadow, blank and dead.

His pencil butted the paper's edge,
sought wider canvases, itched to reach the textured walls
of his room. No longer was he limited to stem
his sketches at her neck, but let grey lines
mould arms and waist, make long legs dance.

He clutched his briefcase tight; its hide turned skin
that warmed beneath his palms. He would hold
his coffee cup as if it were her breast, run his thumb
down and up, stirring its sweetness slowly.
His lunchtime sandwich tasted of her lips;
his mobile resonated with her voice.

Each evening, easing himself from office to car,
he talked to her about his day, asked after hers,
suggested chablis at the wine bar, a quiet dinner;
his happiness complete but for the void
that lingered where her eyes should be.

They broke in when he'd missed a week of work.
It was a shock, they said, to see
those thousand images on papers, walls,
scrawled over books and doors and furniture:
but worse, where arms reached out to beg or give,
they forced his fingers open, found
his own eyes in them, gouged and glazed, an offering
as bright as when they had gleamed from his sockets,
surprised by looking further than his longing.

A LIGHT LUNCH

I always have a light lunch,
my cousin Edward said.

He proceeded to eat
a street lamp,
three light bulbs,
a torch complete with batteries,
two boxes of matches,
a cinema projector
and a large pack of candles.

That's better. Now what shall I have for dinner?
he wondered, eying up the moon.

FLORENCE

The petticoat is old, too small,
she tells herself
while shredding ribbon strands
and rolling them in rough-edged coils.
She takes her rag-doll,
rocks it, croons
'I'll make you better, my brave soldier.'

Little fingers make a paste
of soap and sugar; she gently smears
the mix across a rip,
sees how her poultice holds and cleans the wound.

She learns the feel of bandages,
winding her petticoat scraps,
tying them neatly, checking
they'll not slip or press too hard.

A bed is made inside an empty drawer.
She lines it with cloth,
lowers her delicate child
to rest, cradles its head
as she spoons pretend gruel in its mouth.

No game of chase or June-warmed walk
can tempt her out to play.
She holds the rag-doll's hand for hours,
sings quietly, makes up stories.

When shadows cloud the nursery wall
and lamps are lit,
she strokes her patient's head,
declares 'no fever,' smiles
and drops a kiss where the bandage knots.
'Sleep well,' she says.
'I'll make you better, my brave soldier.'

HEIR APPARENT

He stayed at home for fifty years,
every night set the table,
watched as mother's frenzied cooking
slowed, saw her arthritic fingers
struggle with knives, biscuit packs, bottle tops;
saw that he was trapped.

He listened to his father's tales
with fascination, till familiarity
took over, and he could remember
all the punchlines; listened
to the after dinner snores, grunting proof
the old man still breathed.

Each Thursday in the Red Lion
he would caress his half of bitter
like the woman he had never touched,
rehearse his litany: *No, you haven't won,
it's just an advert* and *Yes, it's still within
the sell-by date.* The irony.

On Saturdays he pushed the trolley -
knew every aisle in Tesco's -
would linger by the kitchen cleaners
relishing the power of *caustic,
not to be taken, may irritate,*
imagining the glug of bleach
poured in the stews and vegetable soup,
basting the beef.

Eighty-five and fit as a flea,
his father boasts one Sunday,
gravy dribbling to the napkin at his neck:
the doctor says I could live twenty years.

He counts the hours on Monday in the office,
contemplates retirement. Twenty years.
At lunchtime he leaves early -
mumbles that he has to get some shopping -
buys a bottle of bleach.

PANDORA

What secrets nestle in your precious jar?
What power do you command?
You, woman,
first and most mysterious,
come bearing gifts of gods.

Fashioned by Hephaestus
at Zeus' behest from earth and water,
you possess Athena's dexterity,
Aphrodite's grace, desire;
yet you are woman, can seduce, deceive.

Guard your treasure,
keep it locked away.

Decked in necklaces,
pearls and flowers,
you bewitch weak Epimethius,
draw him into your snare.

And now, his wife, you need to know;
slowly, slowly open the jar -
learn evil rushing out.

It is too late to catch the sins again.
Earth's balance swings.
You grope your jar's depths,
find one tiny, glimmering gem;
give hope its freedom.

And now you can exert true power,
make your man and all his kind
bend to your will, charm and indulge,
know their place in your scheme.

INVISIBLE MENDING

A coil of cotton slips from its reel,
drips artery blood to stain her feet.
She grips with thumb and forefinger,
forces it through the needle's eye. A coil
of stitching catches her ripped skirt,
anchors the hem, pricks and threads.

A curl in memory waltzes a froth of tulle,
spins under a ball of mirrors,
tears at her sharp heel.
She feels the pull, insistent
as his hand on her arm, his arm at her neck;
she feels the heat of his breath,
weight of his lips wide as a wound.

A coil of cotton twists around her needle,
knots, yields to her scissors' snip.
Her stitches do not show; the gash
is invisible, healed. A curl of horror
rises from her gut, chokes in her throat.

She puts away her cotton, needle,
pins and scissors. Then she winds
the scarlet shimmer of her dress,
wrings it tight, hurls it at the fire.
A coil of sparks flares and flickers, dies,
leaves only snakes of ash to curl inside her head.

TUMBLING

There it is, on a glass table
way out of reach - the shiny key
that will unlock memories
of roundabouts and candyfloss days.
It tempts with Cheshire Cat smile,
but no matter where I search
I cannot find a cake or bottle
enticing me to eat, to drink, to grow.

I try to force the lock on that small door
that leads into a garden
where bean pods bulged in summer, petals
confettied lawns, and a sand pit's foundation
supported moated castles. I can almost hear
the rabbit's mantra: too late, too late.

And now if I crane flamingo neck,
reach a fraction further, I can see
the rounded shaft, precision cut notches,
angled studs, and the gleaming ring
I long to grasp. I can smell
banana-sandwich picnics, tea and lemonade,
the caterpillar's hookah.

At last my arm extends
beyond a memory rush
of party frocks, Monopoly on wet Sundays,
clattering the path in Mum's stilettos.
I seize the key, slide it home, turn -
and feel release of pressure spin through fingers.
I peer at the enchanted garden, glimpse
games of Oranges and Lemons, hide and seek,
the hare and hatter. I can hear
piano practice strains of a lobster quadrille,

can smell Mum's face powder and l'Aimant.

I need to hold each picture, lock it tight,
but underneath my fingers I can feel
a shuffling of cards, can only wait
until they spray the dawn
with red-black shadows, king and queen and knave,
until the key turns and the bolt is shot.

THE RIME OF THE COMMERCIAL TRAVELLER

It is an ancient sales rep
And he lurches up to me.
He holds me with his bloodshot eye -
He's had a drink or three.

He says, 'This wedding is a bore,
So sit with me a while.
I'll tell a tale to freeze your blood,
Or maybe make you smile.

A year ago I used to ply
My wares from coast to coast -
Took bras and briefs and pantyhose
And, though I'd never boast,

Three times I won the Chairman's Prize
For Salesman of the Year.
My car was low-slung, fast and red.'
(At this he wiped a tear.)

'The sun was hot, the window down,
And I was feeling good;
An albatross fell from the sky
And splattered on the hood.

The shock of it caused me to swerve -
I crossed the carriageway.
The traffic cops screamed down the road
And said I'd have to pay.

They said I'd killed the albatross.
The evidence was plain
In fishy smelling blood and guts
And rather gruesome stains.'

I learn he's lost his licence, wants
A lift, leers, 'It's not far ...'
I lie: 'Je suis Francaise, Monsieur.
Je ne vous comprends pas.'

STARCROSSED

If only we could fall in love at will,
could satisfy dynastic hopes and schemes
by marrying to please our fathers, fill
their hearts with joy, but not deny our dreams.
Real life is nothing like the storybooks;
my love will never, never be allowed.
I'll leave without a word - no backward looks -
keep faith with that shared destiny we've vowed.
Together we shall forfeit status, rights,
but count the loss as nothing, for we'll know
days filled with perfect love, ecstatic nights,
as bliss and blessings multiply and grow.
  Our message will endure through space and time:
  I'm yours forever, Romeo. You're mine.

DECEMBER, 1799

Dove Cottage. At times
these past three days, I wondered
if we should ever get here,
what with rain and fog
disguising familiar roads. At least
a fire glows in the houseplace,
though it barely lifts the chill.

Come, Dorothy, a few steps more
and we can stand on Grasmere's edge,
make out the shape of mountains
before night draws her cloak,
make plans for your birthday.

Lake water heals tired feet,
tired minds. Here
we can forge our future
in plain living and high thinking.
Here I shall wander woodland paths,
tell your pen my poems,
work on them at the window
watching as seasons turn trees
from bare, through flowering, fruiting,
to bronze and russet fall.

We will have friends, dear sister,
to visit, share our idyll,
fill these rooms with poetry.
While I labour
you can plant a garden, cook and sew.

The sky is cloud heavy; there will be
more rain before dawn. Let us go indoors,
unpack, transform the old inn
till it becomes our home.

Let's look past Christmas,
make promises for a new century,
settle content in ordinary life,
indulge those happenings which hint
at universal truths. We shall
be happy here.

Take heart, my dear. Soon
winter will shiver into spring.
They tell me that the daffodils are fine.

27th APRIL, 1932
for Hart Crane

'Orizaba' rides the waves,
dips, rises, bearing you
from Mexico's confusion.
      This same water whetted hopes
      just sixteen years before,
      drew you from father's candy
      to fruits of your grandfather.
North of Havana
by three hundred miles,
you feel distance stretching
as the engines throb.
      You wailed no wasteland,
      sung the bridge's hope,
      exulted in your cups.
Blues of sky and ocean
colour your artist's retina,
stir Greenwich Village memories.
      You sold your words
      for other men to sell,
      rooted white buildings
      where chaos crumbled.
At this highest point of sun
your self conceals your shadow.
      Racing to keep in step
      you lost time, fell behind,
      learned Aztec-old cult of death.
Water calls. You remove your coat,
lay it aside, move forward quietly;
leap into the future,
leave your lines to speak.

LEDA'S LEARNING

'So mastered by the brute blood of the air,
Did she put on his knowledge with his power .....?'
from Leda and the Swan by William Butler Yeats

I hardly understand what happened, how
that huge white bird could take me. For a while
I prayed it was a nightmare: but I knew
those strange marks where his bill had gripped my neck,
the feathers in my hair, the pain ... the pain ...
were real. And now I feel a fluttering,
a quickening of child or bird within,
and future fears outweigh the horrors past.
For how can I confide in anyone?
What women's lore will show me what to do?

It seems my torture made me more aware:
my senses all seem heightened. I can hear
a swan's egg crack in nests a mile away,
can feel the earth worms wriggling in soil,
see still pools stirred by breezes, and can smell
lush water weed, and crave to swallow it.

More strange, each hour that passes fills my head
with knowledge people strive for, and the gods
alone should have. Today I understand
the infinite variety of birds,
and start to feel how mountain, copse and sea
emerged from swirling chaos of the earth.
Tomorrow I will know how stars and moon
hang in the night sky; how it all began.
A new fear overtakes me. When I shed
my burden, will I keep this learning? Or
will I become an empty husk, dead shell,
impoverished detritus of the gods?

HEE-HAW

This wood is full of magic -
fairy tunes stop spotted snakes from hissing,
moth and cobweb drift a hammock
for Titania's bed - and I
sing braying songs to warn of day's approach.

But even I was amazed, silenced
when the master's boy
took my noble head and fixed it
on that idiot weaver's neck.

I felt a garland of oxlips and wild thyme
twined all about my ears,
the whisper of fairy fingers through my fur:
looked down to see
a gross and ugly body wrapped
in hemp and homespun.

I could hear
the queen's rich promises of love
fill silky channels of my mind,
spiced with the snap of mustardseed.

I guessed the master would put it right,
clip Robin's ear, bring balance
to the chaos started by that changeling boy.
I never thought
how much the changing back would hurt,
how sharp my anguished bray would sound.

Was it a dream? I'm standing here,
head square on shoulders, my back's cross aligned.
Stamping jolts familiar vibrations.
makes my skull ring as it always did.

But I have been transformed,
have learned frail back, weak shoulder,
know how mortals buckle under love,
know I can never forget.

DEATH BY POETRY

Readers are advised
to be on their guard for marauding packs of poems
that have been cited in this area.
Their weapon is stealth.
They will creep out from their pages
and torment your thoughts.

Sonnets are arming themselves
with sting-in-the-tail
razor-sharp couplets.
Ballads will bludgeon you
into submission. Do not underestimate
the humble haiku; its hypodermic thrust
stings. The poison of a pantoum
will repeat on you, while rondeaus depend
on devilish refrains.

Even though a limerick may lull you
with humour, its final line packs a punch.
Be prepared for the villainy of villanelles,
and watch the shadows where sestinas lurk
with evil intent. Cinquains can stab,
terza rimas suffocate.

If you should encounter one of these brutes
on a dark night,
do not approach. Wait
until the danger passes, and then inform
a responsible editor, who will know
how to defuse it.

You have been warned.